LET'S LEARN ABOUT ALPACA

LET'S LEARN ABOUT ALPACA

by
Petrena Camps

Illustrations by Michael Camps

ARTHUR H. STOCKWELL LTD
Torrs Park   Ilfracombe   Devon
Established 1898
www.ahstockwell.co.uk

ISBN 978-0-7223-4018-9
Printed in Great Britain by
Arthur H. Stockwell Ltd
Torrs Park Ilfracombe
Devon

CONTENTS

WHAT IS AN *ALPACA*?

An *alpaca* is a small camel-like creature. It is a distant cousin of llamas and camels.

A male *alpaca* is called a *macho*, a female is called a *hembra* and a baby *alpaca* is called a *cria*.

An *alpaca* has a long slender neck, slender body, long legs and padded feet.

WHERE DO *ALPACA* COME FROM?

For thousands of years *alpaca* have lived in South America in the high mountains of Chile and Peru. In these countries the winters are harsh and the grasslands poor.

Although it has been recorded that Queen Victoria kept a herd of *alpaca* in the late 19th century, it was not until twenty years ago that another herd was brought over to England. Today the number of people looking after *alpaca* is increasing.

WHERE DO *ALPACA* LIVE?

Alpaca are very hardy creatures and do not suffer from many serious illnesses. On farms they live outside in a field all the year round, with a simple field shelter and windbreak to protect them in very cold, wet weather.

Because *alpaca* are herd animals, two or more must be kept together. They are gentle but inquisitive creatures and make good pets. When they are content they make a pleasant humming sound.

WHAT DO *ALPACA* EAT?

Alpaca graze on grass; they prefer grass to clover. They also drink a lot of water, so it is important to keep their water trough filled in summer when it is hot.

When the females are pregnant, or feeding their young, they are given an extra food mixture to supplement their diet.

In winter they feed on hay, and need a supplement of minerals and vitamins to keep them healthy.

BREEDING *ALPACA*

Each year after eleven months the female *alpaca* gives birth, and she feeds her young *cria* with her milk for five to six months. Very occasionally the mother will not feed her young *cria*, so it has to be bottle-fed just like a human baby.

The *cria* are almost always born before three o'clock in the afternoon. This means they can get warm before spending their first night outside.

The mothers are very caring, and stay in family groups within the herd.

A *cria* will weigh from 6 to 8 kilograms at birth.

When fully grown an *alpaca* will weigh between 45 and 50 kilograms, and it will stand about 1 metre tall.

CARING FOR *ALPACA*

At birth the baby *alpaca*'s weight is recorded.

Twice a year an *alpaca* is given a special injection to keep it strong and healthy.

A check is made on its teeth, which may need filing once a year too. At the same time a check is made on the *alpaca*'s feet, and its nails are clipped if they have grown too long.

These checks are done when the *alpaca* has its yearly *fleece* cut, and details are noted on a record sheet.

The owner also gives the *alpaca* a numbered ear tag and name so that it can be easily identified.

When the *alpaca* is officially registered with the British Alpaca Society (BAS), it has a special microchip implanted.

If an *alpaca* is carefully looked after, it can live for twenty to twenty-five years.

SHEARING ALPACA

Alpaca are bred for their fine *fleece*, which comes in twenty-two colours, from white to black, and every shade of cream, chocolate, oatmeal, ginger, coffee and chestnut.

There are two types of *alpaca*: the *Huacaya*, and the *Suri*. The *Huacaya* has a dense, fine, crimped *fleece*, which grows to about 10 to 18 centimetres long.

Suri fleece can grow twice as long. It is tightly curled and forms ringlets which look like dreadlocks.

They are usually shorn every two years.

In early summer the *alpaca* are shorn, by *hobbling* them between two posts.

The *fleece* is soft, fine, warm, lightweight, very strong and resistant to rain.

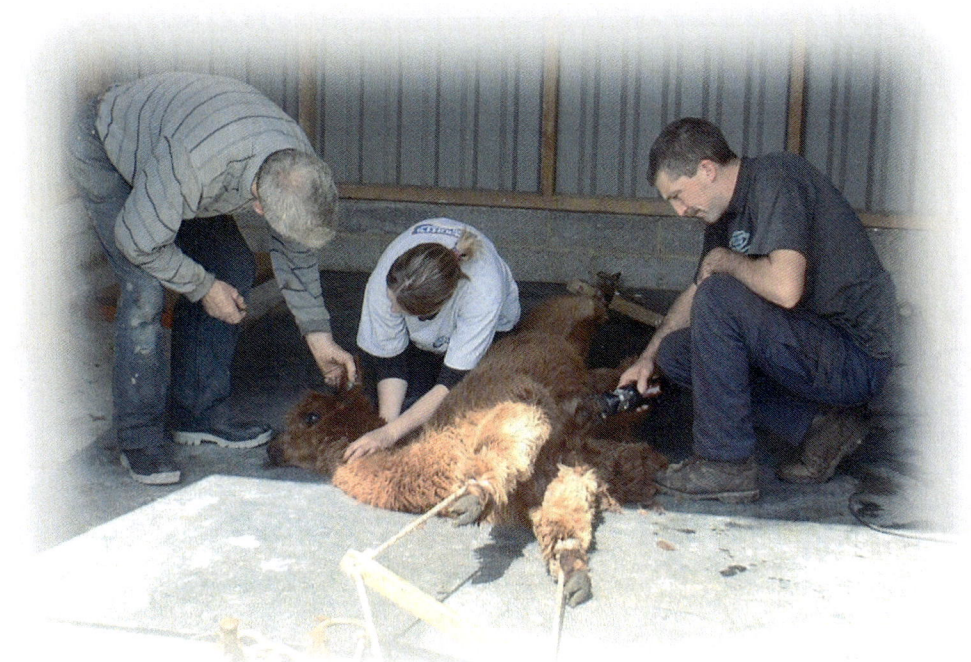

WHAT IS *ALPACA FLEECE* USED FOR?

The fibre, or *fleece*, is spun into thread and made into garments including shawls, scarves, jumpers, hats and gloves. They are very warm and hard-wearing.

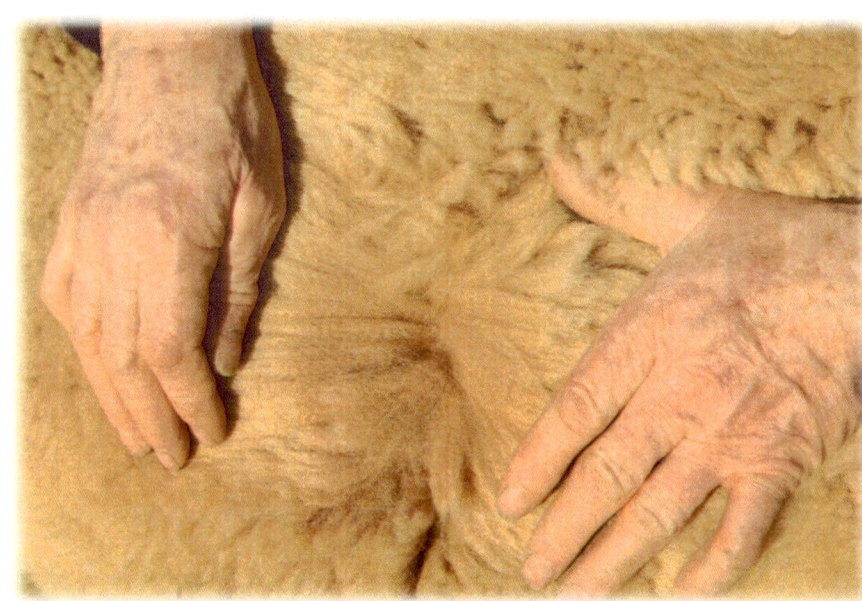

The coarser *fleece* is spun and made into socks or used as a filling in duvets and pillows. Sometimes it is even used for insulating lofts.

Some airlines use *alpaca fleece* for upholstery as it is very hard-wearing and fire-resistant too.

THE FUTURE OF
ALPACA

For those keeping and breeding *alpaca*, there are opportunities for selling animals, *fleeces*, and finished garments made from the *fleeces*.

More and more people are discovering the delights of owning and breeding *alpaca*, so these creatures will become an increasingly familiar sight for visitors to the countryside.

The number of *alpaca* kept in the UK has risen from 150 in 1989 to 25,000 in 2008. Farmers have discovered that *alpaca* are very good at keeping foxes away from their sheep and poultry. During the night when hungry foxes prowl around looking for a tasty meal the *alpaca* chase them away. By keeping two or three *alpaca* a farmer knows his animals are safe.

GLOSSARY

Alpaca   –   A South American mammal related to a llama.   Pages 7 to 18

Cria   –   A baby alpaca.   Pages 7, 11

Fleece   –   The coat or soft woolly covering of an alpaca.   Pages 12, 14 to 18

Hembra   –   A female alpaca.   Page 7

Hobbling   –   Lying the alpaca on its side with its feet tied to two posts, before it has its fleece cut off.   Page 15

Huacaya   –   An alpaca with short, fine fleece.   Page 14

Macho   –   A male alpaca.   Page 7

Shearing   –   Removing the fleece by cutting or clipping with very sharp shears.   Page 14

Suri   –   An alpaca with long ringlets, or dreadlocks, of fleece.   Pages 14, 15

ACKNOWLEDGEMENTS

Our grateful thanks to Rosemary and Robert Gordon for their advice and permission to photograph their *alpaca* at Moorfields Chase Alpaca. Their valuable support has helped to make this little book possible.